MUSIC FROM THE ORIGINAL MOTION PICTURE SOUNDTRACK

ISBN 978-1-5400-5490-6

MARVEL COMICS MUSIC, INC.

Visit Hal Leonard Online at
www.halleonard.com

Contact us:
Hal Leonard
7777 West Bluemound Road
Milwaukee, WI 53213
Email: info@halleonard.com

In Europe, contact:
Hal Leonard Europe Limited
42 Wigmore Street
Marylebone, London, W1U 2RN
Email: info@halleonardeurope.com

In Australia, contact:
Hal Leonard Australia Pty. Ltd.
4 Lentara Court
Cheltenham, Victoria, 3192 Australia
Email: info@halleonard.com.au

CAPTAIN MARVEL

Music by PINAR TOPRAK

WHY DO YOU FIGHT?

Music by PINAR TOPRAK

LET'S BRING HIM HOME

Music by PINAR TOPRAK

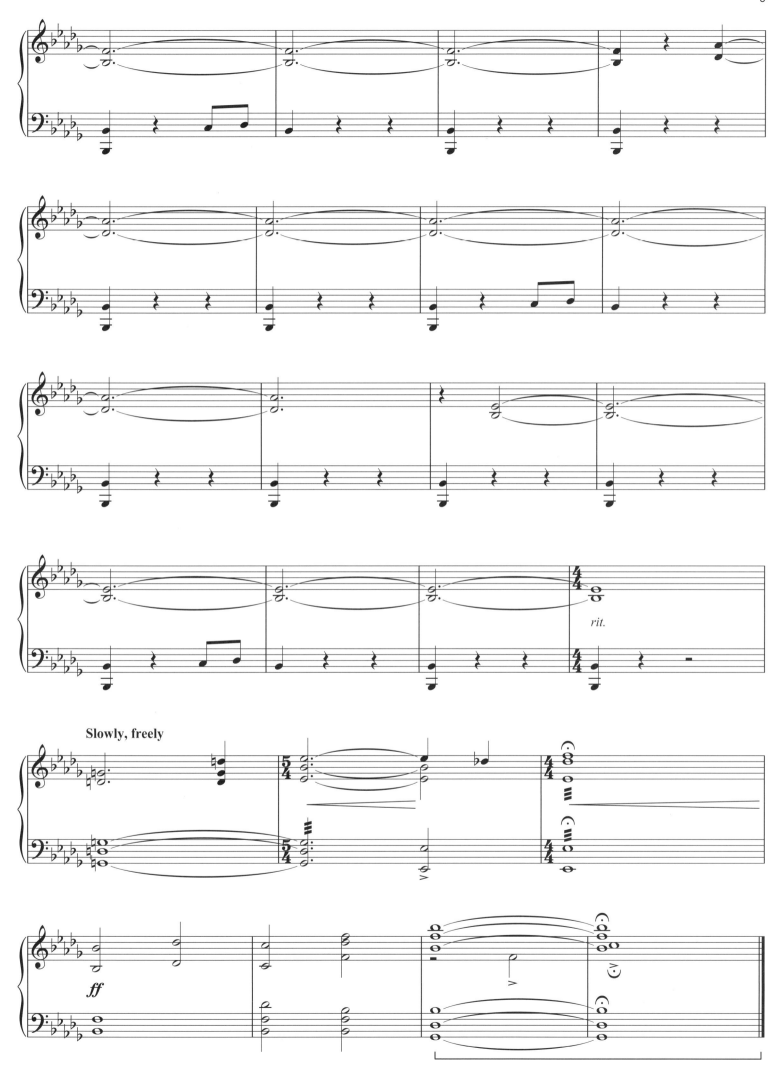

ENTERING ENEMY TERRITORY

Music by PINAR TOPRAK

BREAKING FREE

Music by PINAR TOPRAK

NEW CLOTHES

Music by PINAR TOPRAK

Slowly, expressively

THIS ISN'T GOODBYE

Music by PINAR TOPRAK

Slowly, expressively

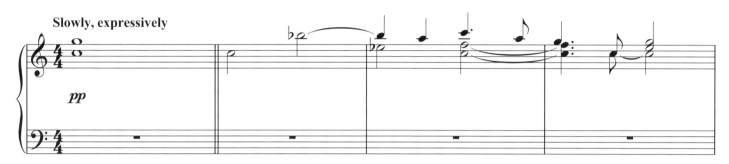

pp

Pedal ad lib. throughout

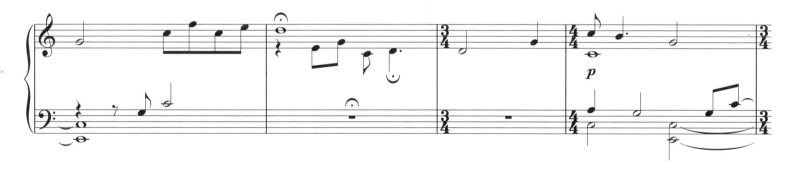

p

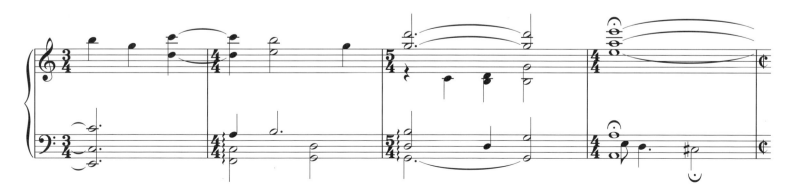

HIGH SCORE

Music by PINAR TOPRAK

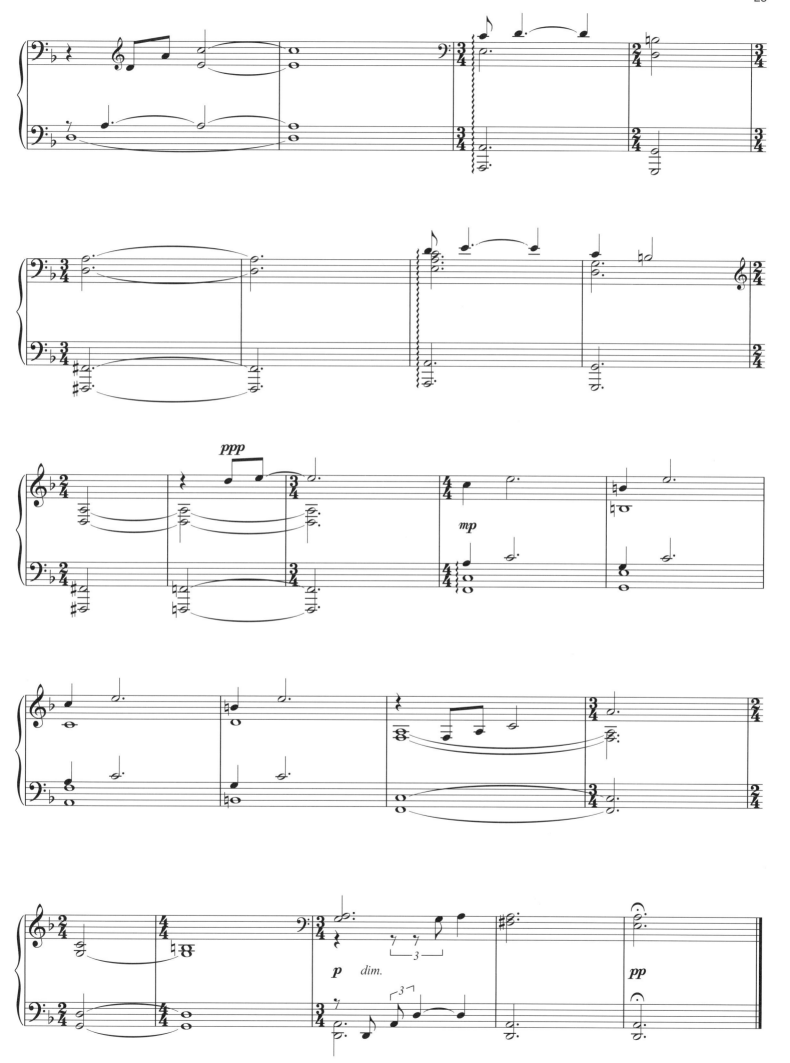